Fragrant Blossoms, Fading Light

Also by Don Langford

In the Light of the Full Moon: Dispersions, Glimpses, and Reflections

Songs from Deep Time

Dwelling in the Twilight Realm

Water Rock Time

Fragrant Blossoms, Fading Light

Poems by

Don Langford

Published by D S Langford Publishing
Columbus, OH 43229
https://dslangfordpublishing.com

Printed in the United States

Cover art design by Don Langford,
Photograph of "Bluebonnets" by Marlene Langford, 2024

Names: Langford, Don, author
Title: *Fragrant Blossoms, Fading Light* / Don Langford

ISBN 979-8-9867546-9-7 (pbk)
ISBN 979-8-9910480-0-2 (ebook)

Library of Congress Control Number: 2024914079

First Printing, July 2024

For Marlene,
always inspiring creativity selflessly

. . . and yet it seems
Life scarce can cast a fragrance on the wind,
Scarce spread a glory to the morning beams,
But the torn petals strew the garden plot;
And there's but common greenness after that,
And what if my descendants lose the flower
Through natural declension of the soul,
Through too much business with the passing hour,
Through too much play . . .

William Butler Yeats
"Meditations in Time of Civil War"

For billions of years
I did not exist.
Then I existed
for a little while.
Soon I will return
to not existing
for the rest of time.

Jessica Amanda Salmonson
"Alive"

Contents

Part 3: 20 Somonkas

About the Author   113

Part 1

Gratitude in an Alpine Meadow

In mid-morning sun
I came around an alpine hillside
to see bright sweet flowers
waving gently, knee-deep, in a verdant meadow.

On both sides of the narrow curving deer trail
cloaking the meadow's softness,
a colorful quiet blanket of whites and blues and yellows
with only the soft humming of bees alighting undisturbed.

This is where I stood for a long while, lost in thought
       or taken somewhere in reverie
       floating weightless,
       protected, warm,
       enveloped by welcoming comfortable indifference.

       All this green vibrant energy
       here before I rounded the bend.
       This place, not here for me, welcoming
       while I pass through the sun-filled moment.

In the relaxing air
       grateful for a place
       life-affirming, slow and quiet

       an inhalation

       sufficient

       enough right here.

Pine Breezes at the Edge of Town

Pine scent
takes me back

small forest in this single tree
spreading out to all the world

the essence of pine
fragrant, out-flowing

uplifting
like a smile
touching the heart

Peace and Strife

Today in the nature preserve
colorful cacti in bloom
birds calling in the trees
hummingbirds trying to have
a peaceful sip at the feeder

Never too far from news
of war and calamity
information traveling instantly everywhere
even inside the garden of peace

Friends gather at sunset
chairs fixed in their westward leaning
soft voices and warm sparks of laughter
into the night

High above, the brightest stars
in the dark desert sky
disguise their turmoil and commotion,
pirouetting in slow motion
like a blanket of stillness
for our comforting sleep

In the morning of choices
we acknowledge the strife and suffering
without drowning in a sea of pain
and see how precious
are the blooms and sunsets
we share with others or alone

The Necessary Occupation

Moving to the edges
of that busy world
and its weighted
         distractions,

there you may find
graceful forms
often at the periphery
         of vision

there to teach
by mysterious
         example

as do warm breezes
         on summer mornings
         in quiet desert
         or pine-scented mountains

birds, too, in their solitary song
         or wild winged flight
         carry with them
         sources of wonder
         to the quiet observing mind

Even the thin green-leafed branches
         windswept and leaning,
         shimmering in sunlight,
         display their learned resilience

But these are not the only examples you need
         to live out the days
         of your deeply examined life

or the reasons
why you move to the farthest edges
of a congested world so difficult
            for you to inhabit,
            and impossible to abandon

the place where the fibers of your being
remain entwined with the conditioning
            that brought you here

When the roots are severed
            and the way back is overgrown
            and unrecognizable,

reaching deep into pools of compassion
in the midst of all the flailing
            and spinning round

can be a lifetime's necessary occupation

Mr. Gullible's Travels

The particulars of his case
                are scant
he left behind so little

spending long fruitless hours
pursuing lives of the sleepers

with their eyes closed
                waiting for some secular heaven

always waking up just in time
                to die again

like a metronome waving slogans
                convincing seekers young and old
                to devote their life to concocting
                other lives all the way back

spitting golden coins onto the sockets
                of eyes asleep or just dead for awhile

Mr. Gullible lived long enough
to see the sacred beliefs
turned to Burma Shave billboards
along the highway of dreams
where the connoisseurs of consumption
converted their restless questions and desires
to a new cult of temptation for others to follow

The disenchanted constitute the new recruits
living at the edge of town
looking for a way to cash it in,
willing to let it all go
if nothing meaningful comes their way

20

And so they seek to overthrow
the madness of the status quo,
hoping to find the alchemy of change
in the dungeons and half-light alleys
where the magical smiles and scented lures
pull them just far enough to bend their hearts

The Way of Memories

Fern tendril unwinding
      in early spring forest hillside
      little green nebulae unfurling

      from seed to root to seed

Your rounded shoulders shimmering
      on the seashore,
      shifting feet lifting sand,
      a smile curving over the horizon

Hardly a cloud today in the blueness of blue,
      memories squeezed out
      in unexpected reminders
      of our quiet walks in sunlit places

We pressed the pressure points to ease
      the pain that had nothing to do with us,
      like shadows following every move

Days like this, so many days like this,
      a thousand glimpses for each shared occasion,
      the flash of fern, feet on the beach,
          your soft shoulders so close
          I could cup them in my hands

With time, the light has bent the recollections,
      reshaped them into shards,
      glistening like electric sparks,
      here for awhile, then gone.

So Glad You Are Here

We live in the shimmering bands
       where light wavers, bends,
            and runs in spectral surprise,

       or spins round like colored pin-wheels
       from old country fairs.

Music of the Renaissance echoed
       for a long time
       in the woodland valleys—
       long lacy dresses,
       children with painted faces,
       the smell of chiseled wood
            struck by a craftsman's mallet.

The fragrance of craft
       stayed with us all these years,
       their talents honed into skills that spread
       into the wooded edges of a country's vastness
       where we find our kindred spirits
            once again
            in our travels.

Here we find soap and honey,
       and there a perfected wine,
       where we spend the night
       at another intersection of lives;
       all of us traveling so far in our lives
            to join for one special moment
            that happens for us again and again.

We did not know there were this many
       kind hearts, working to get by
       and share their talents with others.

What is it that we mean
      in saying goodbye
      with gratitude for sharing
      a moment in the pleasure of wonder,
      a simple exchange of words,
      some freshly made bread and conversation
      before heading down the driveway?

A tiny etching in words,
      carved in light,
      so fragile, almost unspoken.

Contented Little Poet

When the turtle understood
      it could not be a coyote,
      its envy faded

Turtle felt the freedom
      to resume
      being a turtle

Turtle said, "Good for coyote
      to be a coyote"

Turtle could see daisies
      and gophers
      being daisies and gophers

Simple recognition
      from a little poet
      disguised as turtle

Writing little poet poems
      close to the ground
      not in lofty clouds

Seeing simple truths, one at a time
      traveling slowly, carrying home
       place to place, opening gates,
      like little hearts

Turning over little pebbles,
      seeing what lies beneath,
      contented in the little peaceful moments
      as a little turtle poet.

Summer Mountain Hike

Follow the rhythms, the downward easy-flowing swirls,
look for the slant in rock, the leaning shrub and scrub
along the mountain's gully trails
and be guided boot by boot where the horned sheep wander

Rest often, lean against the shady side of rock or tree,
drink in the sun-filled canyon, the quietude, the resting heart
that yearns for the peace and stillness that has brought you here

A sip of warm tea from a thermos in the morning
or a rare treat of dipping sore feet in clear mountain water
before the slant of sun burns the shoulders
and tires the limbs

In these mountains there is no hurry
to arrive anywhere other than where you are
Listen to the breeze and the birds in their morning feeding;
they too are passing through with the rhythms
and changes in water, heat, and food

Stop to nourish the tranquil mind
that remembers for a lifetime
the soothing breaths you took of pine
and juniper on these hillsides
that rejuvenate you each time
you seek their comforting welcome

In the Thicket of Words

In the wooded thicket of words
there are snags and occasional clearings,
confusions and understandings

Around each comforting turn
boulders await, impassable language,
invited trappings of spoken sounds
echoes of lost lives, interrupted pathways,
all the burdens of a world of words

Meanings distorted, wavering in midair, forgotten;
the way the mind unburdens itself
before extinguishing its illusions
in its eroding descent, dissolving ideation

Echoes and shadows, approximations
that never close in on the roots
below the layers of underbrush,
teasing gestures that something
lies just beneath the surface of understanding

The entanglements of the frontal lobe
offering invention and foresight
followed by generations of discontent
no return ticket to enchantment
short of letting go of the mental mapping
one word at a time
        into the wilderness
        of unknown sorrows

New Terrain Arising

We do not cross the keyline
into the domain of a new color world
of experience, unknown terrain,
from which there is a familiar return

No acupressure point or acid dream,
no portal marked as fenestrated entry,
into the already imagined world

Here we swim in the waters
of the familiar
until we are pulled by the tide
of a wider conformity
that we cannot fathom

You will let me know
when a hundred generations have passed
and I am an alien once again
in the tide pools of my beginning

We will not recognize
our naturalized and adopted homeland,
or remember our place of origin

The borders, erased long ago
while our eyes were closed,
mountain ranges erupted skyward,
pushing sea bottom to elevations
beyond our climbing

In a single lifetime
the world becomes unrecognizable,
rolling lava-like, red-hot into the sea,

reshaping old lines of demarcation,
submerging the familiar

Through the rising steam,
new adaptations, fruit flies thriving
in the ammoniated atmosphere,
and gilled neighbors speaking
their fluid signals and warnings
in the amplified noise
of predator-and-prey communication
where restful dreams are fleeting

Fragrant Blossoms, Fading Light

Along the sunny hedgerow
the blossoms open wide,
their petals extending
as the hummingbird's wings
fan the morning air

We see two arising together as one,
a hummingbird flower
giving and receiving
the sweet fragrance of nectar
before the sun's fading light
arrives at day's end

The cows we see grazing on the hillside
eating grasses all day in their slow parade;
we see the grass as milk, converted by cows
as we cannot eat the grasses in all our efforts

In our travels we have neighbors
who arise to noise-making sounds,
news and gossip of the day,
background to their own constant yakking,
loud enough to chase away the birds;
we see sunlight, darkness, and people
converted to a cacophony of electrified noise

We will travel on to see honey bees
abuzz in the wild blossomed fields
and we will taste, with gratitude,
the sweetness of honey that beekeepers harvest;
we see the bees and blossoms and keepers as one,
allowing us the pleasure of the blossom's sweet fragrance
before the fading light of our remaining days

The ocean's sandy beaches
we see as mountains at our feet,
transformed by wind and water and time,
and we, too, in the lens of our own viewing,
we see as the complicated compounds
of all that came before us,
a swirling whirl of energy conscious of itself
dancing for a time as the sweet fragrance
in nature's turning of the sun's fading light

A Day on the River

Old man with bent back remembers
it was easier to break wild horses
in the shallow river water

Downstream a fisherman
strikes a fish's head
against the hardness of river stone
before the cleaning

Inside an arc of orange plastic buoys
swimming children are laughing,
splashing in the sandy shallows
of the river's quiet curve

White pelicans glide
on the blue water's stillness
like graceful boats
floating in the sky

Somewhere a boat's engine goes silent
and two men paddle slowly
with their desperate little fishing nets,
sieves against the afternoon current,
not expecting to be rescued

The shiny silvery blue surface
mirrors the clear blue sky
shimmering where they touch
in a thin band of light—
river and sky flowing together
downhill toward a golden dusk

Morning Ruminations

One lazy warm day, melting
      in their gravel parade, dog people
      tethered to their owners,
      pass in the dusty sun, ballooning blue bags
      swinging from the only free hand they will ever have.

Deer, delicate stepping, through grassy hillside,
      turtles and frogs quiet in the hot creek,
      mosquitoes swarming after yesterday's breezes.

The old man with torn lungs has reached home by now,
      coughing in his red handkerchief waiting to die.

A little girl is telling her father that she has polka dots,
      black starlings on the lawn, magpies squawking,
      tires on gravel, noisy swirling dust drowning the little voice.

Too numerous to name all that is not happening here,
      even the news of emerging despots and tyrants
      tries to penetrate the cool breezes of this hillside retreat.

Dark smoldering clouds hover over the nearby horizon,
      invisible to the blind, devastating as a tsunami,
      a strangler disguised as the Pied Piper on the march,
         whistling into the graveyard.

Do not seek for riches in the sunken treasures,
      this message learned from gold;
      eschew laziness in the guise of contentedness,
      its own sickness of comfort.

Two great craftsmen died on Route 66,
      farmers on acid, witty quiet glances,
      not laughing aloud,

dancing, playful on camera,
coming from music and word-woven skits.

Old memory fragment floats in,
recognized still as memory,
attending marathon Satie piano performance,
metronome on piano, *Vexations* all day.

Someday the mind wanderings
and memories will merge
into one indecipherable flowing present,
impossible to separate again
into recognition; what did they once mean?
What were their origins?

Ten percent of all the humans who have existed
in the last two million years
are alive today.

Imagine a prison, a hospital, a school yard
where ten percent of the population
over the long history of the institution
was crowded into the small space
capable of providing for only a few.

And the effects were invisible to the inmates,
the patients, the children,
the mass of humanity
until smoke filled the ventilator shafts
or the masses were pressed hard
against the chain-link fences,
their faces wearing the waffle imprints
and metal filings
of their confinement.

Sitting in the prison cell, no writing paper
       or reliable memory remaining,
       I try to recall words
       that would stay with me
       if I am ever released:

blue sky
breathe in
       breathe out, yes
       alive
feel
feel something, anything

slowly, slowly open eyes
       heavy, laden by sleep,
       see without naming

this body, seek some glimpse
       of awareness

not too fast, without straining
       feel, touch
       boundaries
       barriers

bones and muscle
       turn to see
       and feel again

hear and see beyond
       this body
       without center
       without walls

sounds from afar
       sights out and above.

Every reverie ends,
the neighbor's loudness intervenes,
the chorus of inner voices and images,
     wispy floating smoke
     vanishing;
my clawing hands in the air
     cannot retrieve the course
     of dreamy fragments

a dumb silence returns
     I slump, like sleep
     overcome by lassitude,

waiting for the next pulse,
maybe a thread to connect
     to some earlier
        something before

When did this happen? Just now.
Just a moment ago. It was here, so close.
What if that was the thought I was waiting for?
The one that would. Think hard. Would what?
What would that one thought have done?

What would any thoughts, the whole menagerie,
     have done, as if you had any choice?

Am I still imprisoned? Who is asking?
     Am I asleep? Is this an exercise?
     Is there anybody there to tell me?
     Is there any me to hear my own voice
        repeating the same words
     to bring back some recollection
     if I just shake it loose?

Through effort, through trying
one routine after another
before the interruptions
send me back down the slide,
the long tumble into starting anew,
so many new beginnings.

To the ground where I lie
        again and again
        waking up each time
        without remembering
        the previous life
                or a moment ago

Voice #1: There is not much time
        between the peak of harvest
        and the rotting of fruit

Voice #2: Let us hope that the poet's long maturation
        is not dismissed by the doddering last days

Voice #3 (interrupting): Like the rotting fruit of old age
        spoiling the long season's harvest.

Voice #2: I was thinking of the backwards projection
        of dementia into all the earlier works, by those
        who look for clues, for signs, for the arc of
        continuity.

Voice #3: Apart from the judgment, what of the poet
        who laid down the markings
        without any intention or foresight?

Voice #1: There is the unfurling of the tendril,
        the imprint everywhere of oak in the seedling,
        of flower contained in the seed.

Voice #2: And does the flowering of the poet
        come laced with decline and insight,
        like light and shadow at day's end?

Even in days filled with interruption,
        consider all that transpires:
        the dew drying, petals folding,
        the paper singed with the sun's flame,
        the fragrance of fire abated,
        the long syncope of afternoon.

Even the interruptions are halted
        so some flow resumes,
        some sense of imagined continuity,
        like this:

Swinging weightless, in a hammock
        floating one way
        then the other,
        windblown, sun warm and welcome
        away from the war and beheadings
        of the counter-revolution,
        away from the fear of the hammock falling
        under the crush of trees,
        away from any thought or counter-thought.

Then the hypnotic spell is broken, a voice, a noise awakens;
        an interruption brings one back again
        to another present moment, waiting
        for another present to resume, to offer reassurance
                for the continuity of desire.

Out of a thousand mid-morning dozings,
        meanderings toward the brink of discovery,
        always one thought away from insight,

thrown back into spheres of memory,
the breath and heartbeat of concentric understandings,
overlapping, interwoven, always out of reach,

teasing and tantalizing attractions, the spells
that await as long as there is a tomorrow.

A faint memory of flowing water,
a river with steep banks,
broken water pipes, a street drain,
rain dripping from a roof
somewhere after a million storms

a resurgence of broken ideas,
caesura to cicatrix,
long curving river scar,
a wound across a nation's belly
the tear in a map on the table,

One thought melting into another
this is the way it will end
all the great minds slowing down,
a sludge containing the best ideas,
congealing in a slow cascade;
the breaking of the machinery,
grinding gears in a soup of foamy thoughts
invisible from the outside
where only the drool on the chin
spittle in the lip's corner where genius once smiled
are signs that the eyes will soon roll back
and tears will arise in the onlooker's eyes

Know these things so you will recognize them
when they arise out of a late dying sleep,
from the purest voices in a fever dream
when all the curtains have been drawn

and the only light is a pinpoint, distant
inside the forehead like some inner door
            waiting to be opened

Insights and interruptions, waiting and moving forward,
            like walking through a lightning storm

In the downward flow,
urgency is the illusion;
acceptance is the release;
liberation as endpoint is the illusion,
stops and starts form the way of downward flow.

Magpies squawking, tires on the gravel,
bring me back to wonder
which has been the interruption:
the outward sounds or the inward ruminations;
            these necessary pulsations,
            acceptance of comings and goings
            allowing the inward flow of fears and desires,
            feeling the downward course of water-flow
                    deep within our innermost veins.

If a Poet Ponders

Tomorrow we set out
        for other destinations;

We know this and we plan,
        aware that we are carrying out
        some unscripted course
        that is not destiny,
        but also not without effort.

The dogs and birds that we see today
        know nothing of this planning;
        for them there is no tomorrow,
        except as today's unfolding
            in the *always present*.

It may be too far back in our travels
        to consider when we were lichens
        or the bacteria that yet guide us from within,
        but it is easier to see in them
        the simpler causes and conditions.

The extent of their planning is their response to immediate conditions.

How complex we have become, driving
        around in devices that replace our feet,
        telescoping the distance of our seeing eyes,
        and wondering where we will eat tomorrow,
        while pondering the many millions who will not eat.

And we have developed the capacity to forget—or ignore—
        our ability to reflect, so distant from bacteria or lichen.

We project ourselves far beyond what we once knew,
        and in our projections and desires

we have sown the seeds of illusion
within the bed of our own hindrances.

*   *   *   *

Walking, gravel sound,
      hear the heartbeat rhythm, harmonizing with breath,
          in step together

Seeing leaves shimmering,
      feeling breeze, the touch on face and arms,
      learning about invisible wind,
      like language.

Hearing bird sound and flutter
      swooping low
      at this *walking I*
      learning protection
      of unseen family.

Hopeless exercise, trying to project back
      before concepts, ideas, words.

Alone on a pathway stone, a poet sits contorted,
      pondering the simplicity
      and purity of a knowledge
         before words, before thoughts.

What kind of understanding was it long ago without words;
      and today, what kind of understanding
      in the vastness of word-based illusions.

How to see the objects of seeing,
      without the intervention of concepts.

What the poet learns from the pathway stone:

    stillness,
        balance (no words)

    gradual flaking away,
    dissolution, impermanence
        (no feeling)

    no perception (no illusion)

The poet does not become the rock,
    or desire to; only pondering what minerals,
    lacking consciousness, experience in their existence.

The poet sees also the tantalizing lesson
    for the metropolis masses,
    dwelling far from quiet reflective pondering,
    too immersed in illusory escape, drowning in ideas,
    grabbing at the delights of their own disillusionment.

*   *   *   *

Of all the possible directions
    that lichens and bacteria could have gone,
    this world of human complexity
    is one of many that unfolded.

How many times the poet awakens,
as if dropped into an unfamiliar world,

        waking again at different markings
        on the arrow of time
        to experience a new alienation

familiar and foreign
pleasant and foreboding

seeing in the delights
an unraveling of contentment

to find in seeking,
the limits of our efforts,

returning again and again
to what matters in the seeking,

glimpsing that everything that arrives
                also departs

all that we grasp on to
                we will release

as do the flowers in releasing the petals
                and the flowers too
                in their own withering
                at season's end

*   *   *   *

Today we settle alongside the wide-flowing river,
        impossible to ford without being swept downstream
        a hundred miles to the ocean; immense repository
                of flowing mountain streams, so much fresh water
                it is difficult to believe it flows in such abundance all year.

And only a few months ago
        in the American Southwest we witnessed
        water restrictions and aquifers depleted,
        residents without water to survive.

We are all the witnesses
to a long-term drying,

veins collapsing in full view
if we do not turn away.

When the poet, painter, or composer
        passes the dry match-stick forests,
        pondering the small bark beetle feeding,
        is there no place in art
                for depicting the slow silent dying?

When eyes are closed
        the slow silent death
        appears invisible

        but it is not made to stop.

And in the silence
        we will observe extinction
        from the inside
        as it happens

and in the pain
        we will witness
        the rhythms of coming and going,
        the largest lessons for us to learn.

*   *   *   *

In the lazy afternoon, gazing simply,
        seeing the sun-glazed hillside
        untarnished by busy thoughts,
        there is the unplanned destination.

Such pleasure, marveling at this moment,
       to be dropped somehow into this present awareness,
       being here to see a deep richness of green
              spread over the breadth of my viewing;

       swaying grasses amid tall flowering clusters,
       small shading trees and junipers and taller pines,
              all sharing a steep hillside that would be a challenge
              for deer or goat to climb, a few small rock outcroppings
              against the deep blue sky, there for all the eyes
              of the world to see, if only they could be here.

And it is here, always, where this privilege lies,
       to glimpse alone, sometimes to share,
       bringing a smile even in solitude, in wonder,
       being able to see all this before reflection,
              before the words and ideas try to capture it,
              and distance that immediate surprise
              of an understanding that precedes the inflow
                     of the poet's adopted craft.

Witness to the Conservation of Matter

The weight of all the flowers
    and the sorrows of fallen smiles
    fall against the mountain's shadows

Evening spreads across the valleys
    we all share, from ancient beginnings
    to the fresh springs that nourish today's travelers

From morning's seed to faded bloom at nightfall
    the imprints of all we know
    are laid in place and then erased

Even the sweetest meadow blooms
    are composed of the earth's oldest ash
    cycled again in all we touch and see

From our love's soft curving lips to the mottled bark of sycamore,
    all are shaped by this earth's thinnest layer,
    coming into view for this moment's eyes

We live in a narrow band of time, with all its overlapping layers,
    able to see with wonder and awe
    the laws contained in the blooms and their necessary fading.

Part 2

Across This Divided Land

Passing through
       the old dilapidated towns,
       with their boarded up windows,
       collapsing porches, burned out attics,

and shredded plastic bags blowing in the dusty wind,
       snagged in the chain-link fences
       and dry leafless trees,

we saw little sign
       of activity,
       none of the noisy sound of construction

that plagues so many elsewheres across this divided land

In our travels
       we have seen beautiful mountainsides
       carved and terraced
       so new homes can be afforded the best views

of an increasingly crowded and congested valley
       where noisy roadways crisscross
       like a scarred tattoo
       on the back of a living landscape

Everywhere, the growing and the dying,
       interwoven,

       people crowded together,
       bringing with them the speed and noise,

clustering in their agitated race to security,
       accumulating what they can
       for some future they will never have

A Ceremony of Purification

There will be love,
        there will be war

There will be compassion
        surrounding a sea of fear

A world that knows familial embraces
        also witnesses flames of fear

There is a pain of knowing,
        and in our wanderings
        we travel with these eternal pairings,
        the twins of suffering and desires for comfort

On the warm desert trails
        with fragrant creosote and inspiring vistas
        we carry with us pained memories
        collected inside muscle and bones
        waiting to be released through effort and tears

We travel these lands
        seeking some cleansing,
        some stripping away

        like the sculptor peeling away the shell
           of a rocklike carapace
           to reveal an inner beauty
           that was always there
           buried in the violence and fear

        that we absorbed and now wish to release
           into the clear blue sky
           and warm desert currents
           in our daily ceremony of purification

Love in the Library

In the open expanse of tables and light, a mother
hugged her daughter for a moment—sincere and genuine,
without asking for any recompense or favored behavior.

Was it instinct or the knowings of love
that caused me to smile when I saw the young mother
embracing her ten-year-old daughter?
And then the impulse to avert my eyes, lest they misunderstand
an old man's grin.

Will the daughter be older than her mother is now before she understands
that instantaneous expression of her mother's love that nearly brings tears
to the older onlooker who has seen so much of it vanish?

In an instant the girl was talking about her exploration
among the books, and the spell was over,
maybe not a moment that will be remembered tomorrow.

But the mother will be there tomorrow to give her girl another hug
and another, for she needs the love as much as her daughter.

An Enduring Ascent

After a long hike to the base,
          the climb up the mountain really began.

At first, no one was present on the gravel trail,
          only the boulders and steep rock face;
          cactus on the ridge line, shrubby trees in the draw.

Then one or two climbers on their descent
          asked if I had enough water;
          offered advice to stay to the left
               on the steep ascent.

A group of three athletic young people
          scaled past me, then another,
          extending his hand and pulling me up
               over a boulder.

"Hey Pops," he called from above,
          "Take a left here; don't go straight up;
               it's too dangerous."

I chuckled as he waved and vanished around a turn high above,
          while I caught my breath and took a sip of water.
          Hey Pops he had said, with such caring and kindness;

               I leaned against a rock and looked out
               over the distant valley, content and safe,
               with pleasure even in the aching breath.

There is camaraderie among strangers hiking toward accomplishment,
          pulling one another along, sharing water,
          encouraging others on the ascent
          an unspoken ethic, shared and passed on.

In the last challenging scramble up the steep ravine
       a gradual curve toward Flatiron
       a half-mile high, level with the distant clouds,
       looking out over desert valley—ancient sea bed.

In the wide flat expanse of the summit, cool gusts unblocked by mountain
       a freshness to mark the end of exhausting ascent.

A sip of water, a few apple slices from the pack,
       hardly a celebration for the hours of climbing,
       before beginning the descent
       strengthened by the knowing that this was done,
a warm and silent satisfaction
that will be carried into the next trail hike
       and mountain ascent
       with new friends to share the way.

Touch Song

The wide range of novelty
touched by song,
       a well-spring of love
       voice of earth-bound friend rising
       to meet in warm embrace

Hand outstretched, fingertips reaching
eyes seeking the coming near
       of musical smiles connecting
       a familiar dancing in the heart,
       soft caresses and desire

These old harmonies return,
reminders of friends here and gone
       heart strings bend in accord
       bathed in sweet fragrance
       soft colors shimmer in the fading light

A Flicker of Light

Human violence is not new
  erupting when food is scarce,
  territory desired,
  power wielded,
  fear mobilized,
  decline forestalled.

The pain of war and loss endures,
  inflicted on generations;
  innocence and hope a common casualty.

So many kinds of suffering;
  ways to break the heart.

Being modern offers no immunity;
  moon landing and atrocities coexist;
  overconsumption and famine
  share the same news report;
  the scale of catastrophes widens.

Behind the numbing statistics
  an individual or family lost forever,
  a community in flames and rubble
  a nation teeters in crumbling chaos

The longer view is not insensitive to suffering
  when it sees the slow human journey
  from savanna to polis
  and all the gains and losses.

It is not naive to say, "Do not feed the wolf
  of violence" or to recognize
  impermanence as a universal truth.

The poetry of awe and wonder is not blind
        to human cruelty when it seeks
        human qualities that cultivate gratitude
            and reverence

        or when we see a flicker of beauty
            in the ashen ruins
            of the only nest we have.

In the interregnum we seek some enduring peace
        that seemed possible before the latest outburst
        or we uncover some poetic fragment
        that reminds us again of our capabilities.

One small voice may not stop the next war or conflagration
        but one heart can touch another heart
        like match to candle
        bringing just enough light
            to see a way forward.

This Determined and Unpredicted Moment

For a time
after leaving home at 14
he worked at the Ford Motor Company
lifting door parts and mirrors
in the long assembly line

then he got a job
driving taxi
remembering all the streets
in Hamilton

then one day
he went into a cafe
for lunch, I presume.

She left Saskatchewan
for the city dances far away
and to work
for the war effort

later she got a job
waitressing tables in a cafe
and one day waited on
a young cabbie

chance meeting
without intent

I wasn't there
but here now
in gratitude
for mother and father

now they are as insubstantial
as before their birth

and I, for this brief time,
catch sight of my own insubstantiality,
events unpredicted and determined
        by all that has come before
        this wondrous fleeting moment,
        this axis at the intersections of time

We, Too, Wispy Passing Cloud

How remarkable, this ordinary moment,
to sit here in comfort
looking to the forested hillside
with clouds passing overhead

The thickness of fragrant junipers
all grown from seed,
windblown or dropped by birds
perched in their own comfort

Over time, through rain and snow,
conditions just right at this elevation,
a forest spread over old volcanic land

We, too, have come out of our own
dust and mud and trees long ago,
and we, as we are constituted,
had nothing to do with the conditions
that preceded us

But we, too, are like those passing clouds,
appearances only, wispy and windblown,
disappearing against the blue background of sky,
returning to the elemental that, too, is borrowed
        for a time

In This Afforded Fragment

And it occurred to me . . .

What if all that remained
was the next eight minutes
of the talk I was listening to

knowing that there was so much more
to the talk that I would never hear

so many more meaningful connections
that I was hoping to make in this life

describing the necessary concentration
that would guide me away from the many distractions,
the unskillful wasting moments,
that can fill the spaces of a life

and if I could remember just one thing
from the eight minute fragment
of the talk with its calm voice fading,
about the natural state of mind
that was joy and compassion
that didn't need to be coerced
or struggled over by effort,

but was like
(now the image of barnacles appeared,
growing on the pier post)
covering over the natural state of mind

still there just beneath the surface
of mental turmoil,
as if waiting

for the presence of a calm and compassionate witness
to its own unfolding,

for some cleansing that would occur
or some clarity of knowing that would surely arise

all within the small fragment of time
that I was afforded

The Music of Letting Go

On secular Sundays we worked,
unstruck by lightning or enlightenment;
memories of karma fields fading
like long broken filaments
releasing their strangling grip,
snapping at our coat-tails.

Like net-less trapeze artists
we followed some unpredicted course
without Olympian gods or their replacements
to guide or counsel us, but we were not alone.

We traveled in the comfort of a long retinue
that came before us, casting off the spells
and fears that spun out from campfire incantations
and mountain retreats softening the psyche
into cultic beliefs of a peace beyond death.

In time we recognized the downward slalom
that we could see everywhere,
the course that the mightiest mountains follow;
so we take the pleasures with the sorrows
and smile at our vanities and desires,
cultivated on the long slow glide
down the ladder one rung at a time.

This is not to say we live in constant mourning
for the loss of hope or striving, because
we do enjoy the pleasures of learning
and the tastes that cross these sensitive lips,
but we do not hold on as dearly
as we once did, willing now to let them go.

In a pool I asked a floating woman
how she did it without sinking
and she said it's the simplest
and most natural thing in the world,
then she bent her head back into the water
and spread her arms and legs
and soon she was resting there atop the water
like a contented starfish in the morning sun.

And in that clear blue mountain light
I could see that the secret
was to place the ears under water
and not listen to the noises from above,
allowing the gurgling from the depths
to be the music of this letting go.

Planetary Citizens

On the long walk home
we see leaves sprouting from
the only tree on the grassy hillside.

As we approach we see more clearly
that among the thickly tangled branches
where swing sets used to hang
young green leaves fan out from the tree's outer surface,
leaning toward the sun.

They are abundant and flourishing it would seem,
but we see, too, that a dry burl has established itself
at the base of the tree beneath the wide branching.

Along the brittle twisting branches,
dry curled leaves look infected
by a canker from within.

The old and drying leaves
are no longer nourished
as they fold and fall in mid-season
from old and heavy branches.

The abundant green canopy
shines and glimmers
in the afternoon's setting sun,
concealing its worn and spreading desiccation.

This was the tree we climbed in as children;
in our common sharing we knew then nothing of alienation
we knew nothing of poisoned homes
or that we risked losing the foundation
of our childhood world.

We claimed no single branch
in our youthful play;
for us the whole wide world,
imagined and real, lay within our grasp.

In those branches we brought
our books of poetry, learning to recite aloud
to the blue sky and passing clouds
and best of all to one another
and to all who were with us
in spirit from around the world.

We are citizens of the world,
abiding by the customs of cafes and bistros,
returning again to these hillside branches
that nourished us in youth,
looking outward, from this spinning orb,
beyond the green enfolding leaves,
beyond the living cloak and dying trunk
that has guided us to the edge
of what comes next.

When the Watchmaker Died

When the watchmaker died
        we wept, not knowing
        whose intent brought us to tears

We thought, at first, the cogwheels of the mind
        would never turn again

Perhaps, through some evil incantation
        the hands of the clocks would cease to turn
        or spin backwards in every town square

With the coils and springs so taut, we were sure
        we were at the gates of the great unwinding

Our numbers had grown,
intolerance and famine sealed off our hearts
        and borders

In a land of parched dreams
reason melted in the unsheltered sun,

What evil genius was behind this, voices chanted
        in the streets, filling the air

Together, we had unlearned so much,
        riding fear to the gates of superstition,
        people branded in the streets
        like cattle, red-hot fire in their eyes

        and amid the widespread carnage
        we were racing to the Moon and Mars.

    *   *   *

Just a bad dream
we told ourselves in the morning

Something had bent time
leading us to believe
in some impending cataclysm
even while we denied its presence

We would walk with a more stooped gait,
and we would never trust one another
as we once did, even amid the jovial laughter,
feigning so convincingly that we came to forget
our own nightmares

for a time.
   *   *   *

Amid the lakes
and the distant snow-capped mountains
one could almost forget there was a world
where hearts were breaking
and life itself was recoiling into extinction

Fragrant sweet clover cut in late spring rows,
trucks loaded with green bales of alfalfa
lumbering along the winding highways
in the golden morning light.

Is there anyone in the fields with their easels
to render beauty and peace in paint or song?

  *   *   *

There were undercurrents
    first of peaceful sounds

tones of lingering sadness
       a violin moving through meadows
       a girl, pensive, standing in her long dress
       her high leather boots secure

    *   *   *

The third generation of explorers
on Mars knew no direct contact with Earth;
       there were few elders
       and no conquest of indigenous people
       to recount or dispel

Their history was a mythology cast in red dust
       revolving around the swirl of cold and dark seasons

No watchmaker or Edenic garden would have been conceived
       to describe such a barren world

Outside the cocoon of their suits and capsule
       a lifeless world of potential called
       for a new kind of adaptation

No pollinator bees would alight on blooms,
       no nectar shared, honey tasted,
       or mead-inspired poems crafted

What words would be shared at such distance
       beyond the practical maintenance needs
       and well wishing?

No more appellation of "beloved friend"
       no epistolary exchanges with earthbound survivors
       no sweet smell of blossoms beyond their helmeted screens
       no more talk of apocalypse among the suffocating captives

*   *   *

To read our poets anew
knowing that not only the books will vanish
but so too the air and water
the very underlayment
of all that we take for granted

The revivification of longing in a time of loss,
knowing that all the fractures and divisions
are nothing in light of the loss of all
that we have come to cherish

The unfolding course flows with an inevitability,
de-centering hominins and all their artifacts

Faced with such understanding, the searing lesson of impermanence,
on a scale that includes the end of everything
do we cherish or will we disconnect;
do we find compassion or burn in flames of ignorance

*   *   *

There are windows through which we yearn to see worlds beyond,
        even while we neglect the comfort of our own musty air

and if by some chance we enjoy a moment in the minty air
        or see a schoolchild jumping rope,
        hear the call of coyotes in the nearby fields,
                or the conversation of neighbors down the lane,

what capabilities there are, waiting to be reawakened,
        to taste in all our discord the sweetness of twilight's nectar
        to look with wonder on the golden light at nightfall.

Revolutionary Impression

[Original oral text attributed to Matthew Collings.
Edited, reformatted, arranged, and poetically enhanced by the author]

Courbet's farmer
      taking a pig for a walk

strolling in the modern world
flaneur and voyeur
poets and painters of color

There is Baudelaire
      creating an aesthetic, an unpredictable blur

and Manet
      visual perception, glimpses
      middle-class artists, weekly meetings

Observe Monet's spontaneity
      expressing movement & light

meeting Renoir
      eating beans together
      dedicated to art

New visual power, formal structure
not painting outdoors

floating restaurant
      in the Seine

the sketch was the real thing

light hitting objects
      like emerging photography
      displaying idealized versions of the world

anonymous society of artists

Impression sunrise
      challenging the relationship
      society and art
      questioning values

From Monet's studio boat
      viewing the play of light
      on water

Renoir's water lilies
far from the world war

reflections moving
purely visual

Cezanne's anxiety
      meeting Zola, the realist
      seeking impact for the ages
         not the moment

in his carefully ordered arrangement
      is the illusion of reality
      fleeting, ephemeral

being real is abstract
      bits of reality based on feeling

transparency and solidity
      approaching the real as an invention
      re-finding structure and order

Cezanne brings restlessness, candor, pleasure
      to the revolution in art

Sleepwalking into Darkness

To be transported
        outside, beyond ourselves
        into distant ethereal realms

This is what we sought
        for those fleeting moments
        spectral and timeless

with a book, held weightless,
        or a movie in a darkened theater
        where all the day's needs
        were invisibly wiped clean

To be catapulted
        out of a dead land
        breeding tiny monsters
        into the comfort of our concrete jungle

Where thought breeds fear
        and artificial intelligence
        rewires all the known circuits
        of our collective consciousness

To be transformed into something golden
        after all the colors had been wiped hue-less
        and every insight we remembered
        returned in jumbled slogans

Take us from our daily dread
        we who take pity on ourselves
        as we pity our neighbors
        with whom we once concocted stratagems
        in the back alleys of our mind

In the panegyric where so many interruptions
        derailed our best intentions
        and well crafted meanings,
        we begged for one single meaning
                that contained all the others

We sought our daily solace
        in believing one anointed leader
        would arrive with flames in his eyes
        and pull on the strings of our deepest hatreds
        and cast our grievances onto the pyre of resurrected miseries

We desired more than all other wishes
        to return to calm and darkened sleep
        where uninterrupted dreams and entertainments
        would numb us once again into accepting
        the fate we demanded and deserved

We were impatient to unlearn
        the wisdom of our ancestors
        and the common civility of the immigrants
                who brought us here

And so we forged in the smithy of our own blindness
        a new nation of sleepwalkers
        who jailed the intelligent, the creative, the forward looking,
        and placed the keys of the asylum
        in the hands of wild-eyed lunatics
        to show us what darkness really looks like

Ceremonial Praise Song

In the dark's egg monicle
luta-brinka foresight

light spondencies tool bricked
fortuna melinka kaloyka

we found gray leyoka seeds
piled agoygka sadeeyo

and in our joy
we forgot seforilda makanoydee

an cried no wayto home,
pleased as poydinka dunes forbinaway
in mild cross-bearings

      *   *   *

Author's transliteration:

We may think we are walking effortlessly
as if we have foresight (and agency)

but there are occasions when we are tool-bricked (non-translatable)
and Fortuna's wheel catches us off-guard (literally, "in our tracks")

we may (incorrectly) believe we have discovered freedom ("found gray
leyoka seeds")
steeped in the Records of the Mountain ("agoygka sadeeyo")

and blindsided, thus, in our joy and fundamental misgivings ("fiorda
baloka")
we lose sight of "seforilda makanoydee" (The Southern Maize Fields)

76

and in not weeping on our way home (ref. to death or Motherland)
we are pleased (honored) to see the "Eye of Forbidden Sand
Dunes" (poydinka dunes forbinaway)
in the mild (or tempered) "cross-bearings" (suggesting our collective
suffering)

Deep Calming Waters

My dear friend—I write to you today
from beside a river that flows rapidly
in such a swift torrent, unrelenting
in its cold movement from the tall
nearby mountains, that its loud roaring
dominates all that I hear.

And I wonder if it is enough
only to describe this river to you,
or if there is a deeper attraction
       and meaning here
         that I should attempt to convey.

I have yet to approach the steep banks
that have been so heavily eroded, revealing
naked vertical earth that will offer no resistance
to any future flood waters that will surely roar
again soon through this curving canyon.

We will remain here beside this river
for five days, and the forecast is for rain
tomorrow, so we will watch for a rising river
in the coming days and see what raging waters
can do during a rapid race down steep narrow canyons.

I hope to breathe the healing mist from these waters
that flow past the hot springs a short distance
down-river. Tomorrow we will soak in the hot waters
that rise from regions deep in the earth where water boils
and gathers minerals on its upward release
through fissures and constant springs.

As one who has not directly witnessed the sacred or magical,
I find there is still a special and mysterious attraction to hot springs

in our travels. I cannot say yet if these are healing waters,
but the body's own intelligence seeks out these warm relaxing pools,
and our fellow travelers always recommend them to us,
as if they know in some intuitive way we will benefit
from the soothing waters, some hot and some cold.

I do not expect a miracle cure
for all that ails me, but the little perimeter
of my world is comforted by the calm and quiet moments
that come from bathing in these special waters.

I will think warmly of you tomorrow from the hot calming pools,
and send good healing thoughts your way.
Don't be surprised if you're overcome
by a deep sense of relaxation
throughout the day.
You can let me know at what hour
you felt a mysterious and calming warmth
bathe over you.

In the Illusion of Self

Each moment
a roll of the dice
not two or twelve, but
       a million directions,
       a million minute, incremental
       influences for wheels to turn,
       opportunities to orbit, winds to blow,
            before an action is taken,
            a decision made,
            a wishful claim to free will and choice

Old spinning orb, throwing out innumerable sparks
along the rails of change, one spark
       landing on this one narrow spindle,
       this one unpredicted outcome,
       this infinitesimal consequence
       of the infinite influences
       pointing toward each single action

And how momentous this one moment is,
realizing that each little intervention
by this person we have become
       is the tendril unfolding toward
            sun and moon;
       the leaf floating downstream
            curling around swirling eddies;
       the genius following its unquestioned path

We are not players on a celestial chessboard;
our roles are not scripted in a cosmic book,
nor did we deserve to be struck by lightning
       or to be born into comfort, riches, or poverty.

In our responses are contained the ten million shapings
        of all the ways we respond to every turn
           in our lives

Where we look for volition, there are the ten million influences
shaping the actions, the responses, the way we perceive
          the conditions in our lives

How we are shaped is not of our doing;
the conditions that precede us are not of our making.
The people we have become is what determines
the way we respond, the way we take action

O' sister, you were gripped so much harder
        than I imagined by the disease of addiction
When you asked how did I kick it, I was wrong
in saying that I just decided to end it, cold turkey.
I did not know then that the millions of conditions
were so different for you than they were for me.
And now I talk to the dead, retelling the stories
of our lives together; understanding now
that you were not to blame for the inflictions
        that consumed you, so young,
           and so long ago

O' son, in the distance the silence of pain,
and in silence the concealment
of so much that might have been shared;
the outer shell holds the scars
        of long-harbored loneliness,
           battles fought alone;
the eyes reflect the long gray days,
        absences accumulated
in a life with not enough love.
Did we run away too far this time?
Did we not try hard enough

to chase you down those early aisles
and share with you more curiosity and wonder
at the wide world we too ran past?

O' mother, who brought me here,
who taught me to please, to seek approval,
to be loved and respected, and who supported
achievements and bathed in vicarious accomplishment,
        proud mother,
        who sought her own dreams
        in the melodies of friends,
my pathetic offering
picked alone in today's meadow of sorrow
is a basket of thorns
when I intended a bouquet of violets,
a painful failure I try to rewrite
        in the poetry of perpetual seeking.

O' father, who taught me by silent example,
the perfection of craft, walking the long straight line
to the goal in winter's snow, finding the coordinates
so easily, using the carpenter's tools for daily use,
I sat for years at the desk you designed and crafted
to teach me where I needed to be in my inchoate craft
of putting words to ideas, as you transformed ideas into wonders of wood.
I marveled at the ways of woodworking, and worked with you for a time
when you rescued me from my wandering, but I did not find as easily as you
the place where I was heading.
In our last shared work together, the wooden railings of impermanence
        held together for a time, while I charted a different course.

O' my Dearest Living Love, my fellow traveler through years of waiting
for a better way, to find now the pains of your waiting,
we seek comfort still in our travels, unmoored from the familiar,
you whose kindest heart you may not see, as others see you,
giving to others and not taking for yourself, except

in the smallest desires and passing pleasures,
I want to give you so much that I cannot give,
except in the glances of gratitude, the smallest gestures,
the brief embraces, and the lightness of shared moments accumulated.
In my quiet and unspoken regrets, I have taken more than I have given,
even in the shared moments where a touch or kind word
would have counted for something.
To my deepest living love, we move together as we did on that first day,
toward some safety in the comfort of each other,
perhaps not knowing where the next day will take us,
but you are the one I want to be with
to share the sunsets and rivers and distant mountains.

Through these loves and sorrows, unfurled in the course of a long life,
the teachings have been contained in the turnings of chance,
the millions of intersecting moments, the unpredicted cascading events,
and all but a few were unremarkable at the time, pushing their way
before the eyes and ears, the tastes and touchings, like a living picture show,
feeding the illusion of self at the center of experience.

And when I stop to ponder that there is no I,
except in the millions of conventional interactions,
there is a whirlwind of dead ends, burrowings in a dark wood
that find no resolution except this:
consciousness emerges, acquires the ability to reflect
within a sea of illusions, unable to find a position
from which to get outside its own limitations;
then, after a time, like all else that emerges,
it vanishes.

A Life of Words Unspoken

Who writes the last letter home
        the hard chosen words
to those erased by time,
their addresses long given away
        to someone new

There was something to say
        long ago
when we gathered together
        in the sun
        that seemed to shine forever

We held our words
        as if their special meaning
        would break like crystal
        if we spoke them to one another

When years had passed
        we forgot what we wanted to say
        and we believed we all understood
            what our gestures conveyed

And now all our unspoken intentions
        rest with us alone,
        knowing all who came before us are gone,
        as we compose yet another letter
            we read to ourselves
            alone in the late setting sun

Connoisseurs of the Dusty Road

We sought the mountains and deserts

Millions of us, invisible,
      burrowing into canyons
      nestling in lakeside retreats
      wearing the coastline painted red
         along our sleeves

Each with our own shining wagon wheels,
      pots to cook in, nooks to read reports
         of distant decay.

We met in small pods, secret societies
      in mineral pools and hot tubs
      where we soaked in hidden waters,
      sharing our ebullient scripted tales

No one ran away in the rainy night, linked as we were
      to the places of our nurturing;
      we were Millet's gleaners, the grazers,
      connoisseurs of the dusty road,
      curious in our wandering ways, sharing
      furtive glances under the cover of bubbling waters.

We shared our ignorance and wisdom,
      our mistakes that pushed us forward,
         and then we parted.

We grew accustomed to the welcoming smiles,
      parting footsteps in our unacknowledged melancholy,
      knowing these intersections of lives,
      the slow pummeling of the road
         toward a curved horizon,
         the taste of letting go.

Five Gates of Entry

Long papery snakeskin sheets
draped atop old rusted wire fence,
shimmering desert heat,
tumbleweed skeletons blowing to silent snow
on distant mountains

My eyes rest quietly on the scene
seeing the story of Snake
climbing barbed wire fence
rehearsing for the climb up
distant snow-capped mountain

Or shot for sport and wrapped about
the top barbed strand as trophy or warning
to other snakes who might seek tall mountains

The story did not end well for Snake
so I must turn away to reinvent
the journey, so Snake does not stare in death
at the lofty mountain peaks
eternally out of reach

I, too, feel the mysterious pull of the mountain peak
and the gates and trials I must pass through
as if Snake had one more chance
in the guise of a little old poet
or desert hermit devoted to his craft
of recording how the journey unfolds

One by one the five gates offer openings
to the trail leading ahead,
learning more the modest craft,
receiving more the opportunities
of dwelling a little longer

on the trail leading from base toward summit
or to the vistas along the way
that offer their own rejuvenating reward

So I unwind Snake's dried skin,
flakes breaking off in my hands,
placing fragments and powdery remains
carefully in the small pouch I will carry
at my side, and if I speak aloud at times
in my travels forward, it is so Snake will hear
that we travel together on this noble path,
and when I am silent, it is so I can listen
to Snake's guiding wisdom

Part 3: 20 Somonkas

The Somonka style of poetic expression, like the more familiar haiku, has a structure based on the number of syllables contained in the lines. However, unlike the haiku, the Somonka consists of two stanzas called tankas, written as if by two individuals, one answering the other typically in a romantic exchange. Each tanka contains five lines with a syllable count of 5, 7, 5, 7, 7.

Somonka 1

From this wild canyon
leaping airborn for your love
it seemed possible
that I could glide all day long
waiting for you to join me

From river bottom
I watched you soaring above
pulling my heart upward
to join again in mid flight
as we do each time I dream

Somonka 2

Far from home I go
where white lotus blossoms grow
in deep blue water
opening in bright sunlight
a pond of smiling faces

I too see the sun
standing with my arms outstretched
a cup of hot tea
simmers for your safe return
bring your sweet smile home to me.

Somonka 3

In the summer night
glowing fireflies fill the sky
each one a love note
a tiny caress for you
from my open heart to yours.

Searching for nectar
the hummingbird stays aloft
throughout the long day
patient for the love that waits
gratefully at end of day.

Somonka 4

With you beside me
I seek the quiet places
away from the crowds
in the coolness of rivers
or the mountains and deserts.

I am ready now.
The journey will be our home.
This will be the dream
that we have planned for so long.
It is time for us to go.

Somonka 5

Pleasant to sit here
on the forest path with you.
Even with eyes closed
there is joy when you are near.
Sunlight breaks through misty fog.

When I see these trees
I am renewed once again.
Let's cherish this time
that brings us together here
among ancient wooded pines.

Somonka 6

On this sandy shore
with a basket of ripe plums
we sat years ago.
Now we return much older
to taste the sweetness of time.

Our little bounty
was always enough for us.
Who could ask for more?
Hearts grow in places like this
with warm waves of gratitude.

Somonka 7

Walking this canyon
lost in peaceful thoughts with you,
sun shining through clouds,
fragrant scent of cypress pine,
I can ask for nothing more.

The sky has opened
casting streams of light downward;
around the next bend
our warm water pool awaits
to sooth and refresh our minds.

Somonka 8

Wheels fall off the cart,
mud flies in all directions,
the going gets tough.
Each new day we move forward,
mending wheels along the way.

Some days seem so dark
even you sadden my heart.
Somehow we move on
in our own isolation,
each seeking the other's love.

Somonka 9

Using rake and hoe
cultivate the simple life
For years we tilled soil
preparing a small seedbed
now we harvest peaceful days

It's our good fortune
to have these days together
after years of toil
we roam the land in comfort
no longer tied to a place

Somonka 10

On warm canyon rim
seated on rock facing sun
silent end of day
sharing this moment with you
who are never far away

Out of the silence
ravens call in the valley
I hear them from here
They remind me of our song
far away and very near

Somonka 11

Much like the turtle
we carry our home with us
following the sun
seeking the quiet places
taking only what we need

We are fortunate
to be traveling like this.
When we hear the noise
we bundle up and move on
where peace and sun await us.

Somonka 12

Like nomads we roam
sometimes on the flat land route
other times we climb
up Superstition Mountain
looking down from Flatiron

I am resting here
with a book and looking up
you say you see me
down here on safe ground waiting
wishing to be there with you

Somonka 13

If I was the sky
spreading a blanket of stars
followed by sunlight
all your days would be peaceful
after rising each morning

If I was the earth
holding the warmth of your glow
we could pass the time
dancing in each others arms
inviting all to join us

Somonka 14

Like innocent child
I picked a bouquet for you
Tiny marigolds
When you deserved a garland
Please accept my best intent

From your heart to mine
Loving intentions arrive
I accept your love
Little yellow sea flowers
And our sand dune memories

Somonka 15

In filtered sunlight
you radiated such love
your red hair glittered
and my world lit up brightly
knowing you were close to me

In one another
we see the light that joins us
shining sun and glow
radiant and selfless love
always there for us to share

Somonka 16

I picked this flower
a gift of color for you
knowing it will fade;
please accept it from me
a token bloom of my love

The color may fade
and petals may drop away
but for this moment
the flowering of our love
waves freely in the sunlight

Somonka 17

There are those who say
true love will last forever
but if the sun sets
and every season ends
let us not squander our love

We know that love grows
some like redwoods, some like pines
and what starts must end
so we value what we have
in this one precious moment

Somonka 18

In time we have learned
there is kindness all around
like lotus flowers
that bloom on peaceful waters
there for everyone to see

During our travels
we have found many people
who share our desires
for peaceful and modest lives
lucky to attract like minds

Somonka 19

We reflected long
before adopting travel
as a way of life.
Each day I am rewarded
seeing the country with you.

Waking up each day
I get to see something new.
The greatest comfort
is knowing you are with me
living our dream on the road.

Somonka 20

One sure mystery
as we travel together
is never knowing
how or when the journey ends
so we live each day in love

Something we have learned
in these many years
is the importance
of confiding truthfully
and letting our love guide us

About the Author

Don Langford is a little poet
who travels, writes his poems,
and is often reminded
by the world around him
that the one he loves
has been with him all this time
bringing gratitude to the surface,
teaching patience by her presence.